SPORTS SUPERSTARS

ANTONIO BROWN

By Anthony K. Hewson

Kaleidoscope
Minneapolis, MN

Your Front Row Seat to the Games

This edition is co-published by agreement between Kaleidoscope and World Book, Inc.

Kaleidoscope Publishing, Inc.
6012 Blue Circle Drive
Minnetonka, MN 55343 U.S.A.

World Book, Inc.
180 North LaSalle St., Suite 900
Chicago IL 60601 U.S.A.

Kaleidoscope ISBNs
978-1-64519-097-4 (library bound)
978-1-64494-192-8 (paperback)
978-1-64519-136-0 (ebook)

World Book ISBN
978-0-7166-4338-8 (library bound)

Library of Congress Control Number
2019940055

Printed in the United States of America.

TABLE OF CONTENTS

CHAPTER 1

A Timely Score

Antonio Brown starts to run his **route**. The game is on the line. Less than fifteen seconds remain. His Pittsburgh Steelers trail the Baltimore Ravens by three. Now they need a score.

Brown knows he needs to be exact with his route. He runs straight for one yard. Then he cuts to his right two yards. He's right where he needs to be. The pass comes right to him. Now he turns toward the end zone. It's just two yards away. But a pair of Ravens defenders are in the way.

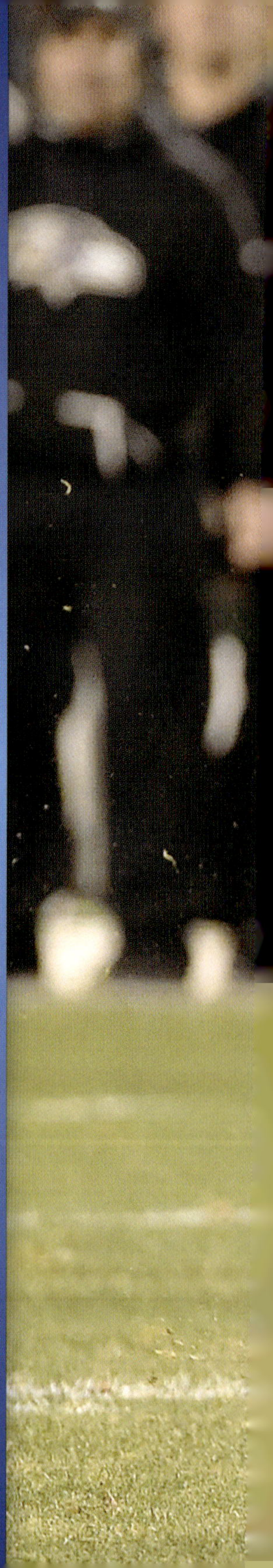

Antonio Brown and the Steelers had much to play for in their 2016 game against the Ravens.

Brown stretches as far as he can to try to reach the end zone.

The defenders slam into Brown. He slams right back into them. One defender wraps Brown up. The Steelers receiver can barely move. But he never stops trying. He pushes. Then he pushes some more. Then he goes for it.

Brown stretches his arm out. He reaches as far as he can. The Ravens don't give in. They push and push. Finally they drive Brown back. But it's too late. The ball had crossed the goal line. The referee raises his arms. Touchdown! The Steelers held on to win 31–27. Then the celebration began in Pittsburgh.

FUN FACT

Brown scored 79 touchdowns from 2010 to 2018. Of those, 20 came in the final two minutes of a game.

The Ravens are a **rival**. Any win over them is big. But this win was extra important. It secured a spot in the playoffs. Brown's touchdown was the difference.

By 2016, Brown was one of the most feared wide receivers in the National Football League (NFL). That wasn't always the case. He had to work hard to become one of the league's best receivers.

THE IMMACULATE EXTENSION

Brown's winning touchdown became known as the "Immaculate Extension." The nickname refers to another famous Steelers play. In 1972, Pittsburgh won a game with a miracle catch for a touchdown. That play is known as the "Immaculate Reception." Both nicknames are based off a story from the Bible.

Brown's game-winning touchdown led Pittsburgh to the playoffs.

CAREER TIMELINE

1988

July 10, 1988
Antonio Brown is born in Miami, Florida.

2007

2007
Brown arrives at Central Michigan University, where he joins the football team.

2010

January 6, 2010
Brown scores touchdowns on a run and kick return in his final college football game.

April 24, 2010
The Pittsburgh Steelers select Brown in the sixth round of the NFL **Draft**.

2010

September 19, 2010
Brown scores his first NFL touchdown on a kickoff return against the Tennessee Titans.

2011

February 6, 2011
Brown goes to the Super Bowl in his first year with the Steelers, but they lose to the Green Bay Packers.

2012

January 29, 2012
Brown plays in his first Pro Bowl.

2016

December 25, 2016
In a game against the rival Baltimore Ravens, Brown scores a game-winning touchdown to send Pittsburgh to the playoffs.

2019

March 10, 2019
The Raiders trade for Brown.

CHAPTER 2

Finding Success

Antonio Brown stepped onto the football field. He felt right at home. His dad Eddie threw a pass. Antonio caught it. Then he passed to his younger brother, Desmond. As a kid, Antonio spent hours on the field. He loved having fun and playing with his dad and brother.

Antonio spent many hours playing football with his dad and brother growing up.

Eddie was a **professional** football player. He played in the Arena Football League. Antonio and Desmond visited him. Sometimes they even went to his practices. However, they lived mostly with their mother, Adrianne. The family didn't have much money. Antonio was born on July 10, 1988, in Miami, Florida. That's where he grew up.

Miami, Florida

FUN FACT

Antonio grew up 1 mile (1.6 km) from fellow NFL receiver T. Y. Hilton.

Antonio lined up behind the center. He was playing quarterback. But that was just one of his positions. He also played running back. He was a wide receiver. He returned kickoffs and punts, too. Antonio played five positions through high school. And he played all of them really well.

Football was an escape for Antonio. His neighborhood had a lot of crime. Football helped him stay safe. It helped that Antonio was a star. He could run really fast. The next step was to play in college. There was one problem. Antonio didn't have good grades. Many schools rejected him. Eventually, he went to Central Michigan University. It wasn't a big school. But Antonio saw opportunity there.

Antonio was determined to make the most of his opportunity at Central Michigan.

FUN FACT

During Antonio's first season at Central Michigan, he played wide receiver while future NFL defensive lineman J. J. Watt played tight end for the team.

Antonio sprints across the field. The quarterback hands him the ball. Antonio races toward the end zone. He has 10 yards to go. No problem. He crosses the goal line for the touchdown.

Later, Antonio catches the kickoff. He begins running. But no one is near him. All the defenders are blocked. He runs 95 yards all the way to the end zone. Touchdown!

Antonio makes a big catch during the GMAC Bowl.

In college, Antonio continued to play two positions. He was a wide receiver. He also returned kicks. And just like in high school, he was really good at both.

That showed in his final college game. Central Michigan was selected to play in the GMAC Bowl. It was a high-scoring game against Troy University. Antonio scored two touchdowns. Then he was off to the NFL.

CHAPTER 3

Giving Back

Antonio Brown held a game controller. Next to him was a boy. He was a **patient** at the Pittsburgh Children's Hospital. He had a controller, too. They faced off in a football video game. Brown spent time meeting with other sick kids there.

Brown talked to every kid he could. They took selfies. Brown brought pizza. He told the kids to have a good attitude. Everyone smiled. Life can be challenging for these kids. Brown's visits help cheer them up. He likes visiting. Brown said helping kids is more important than football.

Brown spent nine seasons in Pittsburgh, Pennsylvania.

Brown always makes a point to give back to fans.

Where Brown Has Been

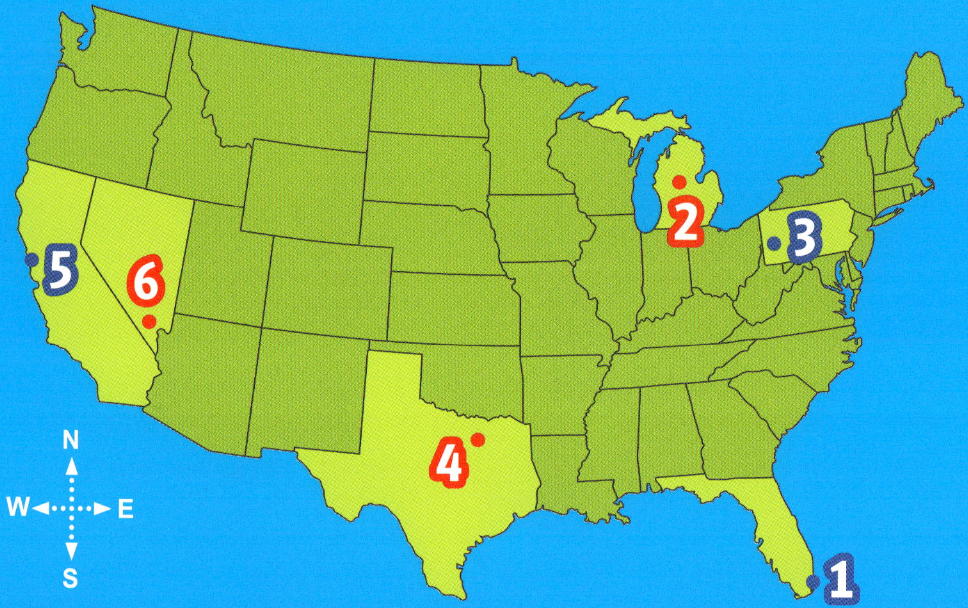

1. **Miami, Florida:** Brown was born here.
2. **Mount Pleasant, Michigan:** The home of Brown's college team, the Central Michigan Chippewas.
3. **Pittsburgh, Pennsylvania:** Brown played here with the Steelers from 2010 to 2018.
4. **Arlington, Texas:** During Brown's first NFL season, the Steelers reached the Super Bowl but fell to the Green Bay Packers.
5. **Oakland, California:** The Steelers traded Brown to the Raiders after the 2018 season.
6. **Las Vegas, Nevada:** The Raiders planned to move here in 2020.

Brown arrived at a school. He brought 800 backpacks. Each was filled with school supplies. Brown's family didn't have much money when he was growing up. He couldn't afford to buy much. He knew some kids in Pittsburgh faced the same challenges. So he brought them backpacks.

"I want to make a difference," he said.

Another time, Brown visited a Pittsburgh **food bank**. He packed boxes full of food. The boxes went to families who couldn't afford groceries. Brown donated 5,000 bowls of soup to the food bank. It's another way Brown helps those in need.

FUN FACT

In 2017, Brown hosted a charity basketball game that featured athletes and celebrities such as DJ Khaled and Tracy McGrady.

A photo appeared on Instagram. It showed Brown. He was throwing a **medicine ball**. That was part of his offseason training. Brown spends a lot of time working out. He also uses social media a lot. He posts several photos per day. This gives fans a chance to connect with him.

Another time, Brown competed against fellow NFL player Von Miller. But this time, there was no football involved. They were on *Dancing With the Stars*. However, neither won the TV show's spring 2016 season.

Brown wasn't done on TV. In 2019, he was back. This time he was on *The Masked Singer*. He dressed up as a hippo. He sang a song. But he was eliminated right away! Many fans know Brown for his football skills. These appearances help him connect with more fans.

FUN FACT

Brown appeared with rapper Drake in the music video for the song "God's Plan."

Brown and soccer star Alex Morgan presented an award at the 2018 ESPY Awards.

CHAPTER 4

Brown runs back the opening kickoff in his first NFL game.

Becoming A Star

The kicker sent the ball flying. It landed in Brown's hands. And he was off. The opponents moved fast. But Brown was faster. He scanned the field. He saw an opening. Then he raced through it. He didn't stop until he scored a touchdown. It was an 89-yard return. And it came in Brown's first game with the Pittsburgh Steelers.

Some doubted Brown would ever play in the NFL. The Steelers took a chance on him. They selected him in the 2010 draft. But it wasn't until the sixth round. They believed he could be good. But he would need time. As a **rookie**, Brown mostly returned kicks and punts.

FUN FACT

Twenty-one wide receivers were taken in the NFL Draft before the Steelers drafted Brown in 2010.

Most of the Steelers had left the practice field. Not Brown. He remained. So did a few teammates. They wanted more work. So Brown ran routes. He caught passes. Then he did it again. Brown wanted to be a star. So he worked really hard. Even Steelers coach Mike Tomlin was impressed.

The hard work paid off. Brown became a starting receiver by 2011. Soon after he became a star. Brown was **consistent**. This helped him earn the coaches' trust. The more he played, the better he got. Before long he was one of the best receivers in the league. Some have said he is among the best ever.

FUN FACT

Brown caught more than 100 passes each season from 2013 to 2018.

Brown put in a lot of practice before becoming a superstar.

CAREER

STATS

Through the 2018 season

GAMES PLAYED	130
CATCHES	837
YARDS PER GAME	86.2
TOUCHDOWN CATCHES	74
RETURN TOUCHDOWNS	5

Brown was eager for a fresh start with the Raiders.

Steelers fans stood and cheered. Brown had just scored a 47-yard touchdown. It was one of two he scored that day. The fans could relax. Pittsburgh was on the way to an easy win over the Atlanta Falcons. But Brown wasn't so happy. He was playing well. But he wasn't getting along with his coaches and teammates.

He asked to be traded. Some people said he gave up on the team. But Brown believed in himself. Finally, after the season, it was over. The Raiders traded for Brown. They were preparing to move to Las Vegas. Brown was getting a fresh start. The Raiders were getting a new star.

BEYOND THE BOOK

After reading the book, it's time to think about what you learned. Try the following exercises to jumpstart your ideas.

THINK

THAT'S NEWS TO ME. Brown requested a trade from the Pittsburgh Steelers after the 2018 season. How might news sources be able to fill in more detail about this? What new information could you find in news articles? Where could you go to find those sources?

CREATE

SHARPEN YOUR RESEARCH SKILLS. Brown played for a small university, Central Michigan. Where could you go in the library to find more information about Brown's college football career? Who could you talk to who might know more? Create a research plan. Write a paragraph about your next steps.

SHARE

SUM IT UP. Write one paragraph summarizing the important points from this book. Make sure it's in your own words. Don't just copy what is in the text. Share the paragraph with a classmate. What questions does your classmate have about the summary?

GROW

REAL-LIFE RESEARCH. What places could you visit to learn more about Brown? What other things could you learn while you were there?

RESEARCH NINJA

Visit www.ninjaresearcher.com/0974 to learn how to take your research skills and book report writing to the next level!

RESEARCH

DIGITAL LITERACY TOOLS

SEARCH LIKE A PRO
Learn about how to use search engines to find useful websites.

FACT OR FAKE?
Discover how you can tell a trusted website from an untrustworthy resource.

TEXT DETECTIVE
Explore how to zero in on the information you need most.

SHOW YOUR WORK
Research responsibly—learn how to cite sources.

WRITE

GET TO THE POINT
Learn how to express your main ideas.

PLAN OF ATTACK
Learn prewriting exercises and create an outline.

DOWNLOADABLE REPORT FORMS

Further Resources

BOOKS

Fishman, Jon M. *Antonio Brown*. Lerner Publications, 2019.

Monnig, Alex. *Antonio Brown: Football Star*. Focus Readers, 2018.

Whiting, Jim. *The Story of the Pittsburgh Steelers.* Creative Education, 2019.

WEBSITES

FACTSURFER

Factsurfer.com gives you a safe, fun way to find more information.

1. Go to www.factsurfer.com.
2. Enter "Antonio Brown" into the search box and click 🔍.
3. Select your book cover to see a list of related websites.

Glossary

consistent: Someone is consistent if he or she does something regularly. Brown was consistent in catching passes during games.

draft: Pro sports teams use a draft to choose new players to add to their rosters. The Pittsburgh Steelers chose Brown in the sixth round of the 2010 draft.

food bank: A food bank is a place that serves food to those who cannot afford it. Brown handed out bags of groceries one afternoon at the food bank.

medicine ball: A medicine ball is a heavy ball used during workouts. Brown tossed a medicine ball to build up his strength.

patient: A patient is someone being cared for by a doctor. Brown visited hospital patients and played video games with them.

professional: To be professional means to be paid for doing something. Antonio's dad, Eddie, played professional arena football.

rival: A rival is a player or team you're competing against often for the same prize or reward. The Steelers and Baltimore Ravens play each year and are rivals.

rookie: A rookie is a player in his or her first year in a new league. Brown spent his rookie NFL season developing his skills.

route: A route in football is the path a wide receiver runs to get open during a play. Brown runs his route to get open and catch a pass.

Index

PHOTO CREDITS

The images in this book are reproduced through the courtesy of: Matt Patterson/AP Images, front cover (center), front cover (right), p. 3; EFKS/Shutterstock Images, front cover (background bottom), front cover (background top); Jeff Bukowski/Shutterstock Images, pp. 4, 9 (bottom); Fred Vuich/AP Images, pp. 4–5, 6–7; Don Wright/AP Images, p. 8; Joe Belanger/Shutterstock Images, pp. 9 (top), 30; Red Line Editorial, pp. 9 (timeline), 18, 25 (chart); FloridaStock/Shutterstock Images, p. 10; Anil Gurcay Dede/Shutterstock Images, p. 11; Al Goldis/AP Images, pp. 12–13; Rogelio V. Solis/AP Images, pp. 14–15; Sean Pavone/Shutterstock Images, p. 16; Steve Luciano/AP Images, p. 17; Billion Photos/Shutterstock Images, p. 19; Phil McCarten/Invision/AP Images, pp. 20–21; Robert Smith/The Leaf-Chronicle/AP Images, pp. 22–23; Keith Srakocic/AP Images, p. 24; Gene J. Puskar/AP Images, p. 25 (Antonio Brown); Ben Margot/AP Images, pp. 26–27; LunaseeStudios/Shutterstock Images, p. 27.

ABOUT THE AUTHOR

Anthony K. Hewson is a freelance writer originally from San Diego, now living in the Bay Area with his wife and their two dogs.